Half Breed: My Personal Journey to Freedom
ISBN: 978-1-7341346-6-7

LOC Control #: 2020905829

Copyright © Jaclyn Lowe

Publisher and Editor: Fiery Beacon Publishing House

Fiery Beacon Consulting and Publishing Group

This work was produced in Greensboro, North Carolina, United States of America.
All rights reserved under International Copyright Law. No portion of this publication may be reproduced, stored in any electronic system or transmitted in any form or by any means (electronic, mechanical, photocopy, recording or otherwise) without written permission from the publisher or author, Jaclyn Lowe. Brief quotations may be used in literary reviews. Unless otherwise noted, all scripture references have been presented from the New King James version or Amplified version of the bible.

Half – Breed

My Personal Journey to Freedom

By

Jackie Lowe

TABLE OF CONTENTS

The Dedication
The Forward

The Dedication

First I would like to thank God for his ferocious love that never allows me to quit. This book is solely out of my willingness and obedience to Him.

I want to thank my mother, Janice Pavy. Thank you for your God given mother's love. I am so grateful that God chose you to be my mother. You taught me how to serve with love and grace, no matter the cost.

To my dad John Vernon thank you for always challenging me. You opened me up to a whole new life and a whole new way of thinking. I am honored to be your daughter.

To my loving husband Bryan Lowe. Thank you for your faithfulness to me. I was a broken girl when we met, and you remained by my side. We literally grew up together. The love that God gave you for me is priceless and in return we have built a beautiful life, family, and ministry together. Thank you for not allowing me to quit on myself.

To my beautiful kids Jaquel, Jaryn, Bryson, and Eliana Grace - Thank you for stretching me and causing me to grow in so many different ways. I am blessed to be your mother. I pray that my life will always point you back to the love and grace of God. I love you more than you will ever know.

To my dearest sister who would kill me if I put her name. We may not be blood related sisters, but we are truly Blood Sisters. From day one, we have been Kingdom Connected. Thank you for accepting me and allowing me to be me. Thank you for the ability to be able to handle all of me. I am forever grateful to God for sending me you.

To my aunt and mentor Angelena Vernon, what can I say except Thank You God for connecting us. Through God, you have discipled me and helped me navigate the prophetic realm. Your stewardship to God has helped trained me up more than you will ever know. Your life is a living testimony of how Great our God is!

To Freedom Ministries Church and Outreach - Wow thank you for pushing me and for continuing to help me discover new levels within myself!

Thank you to Pastor Brandi Rojas of Fiery Beacon Publishing – My "Go Forth" Sister Thank you for being the midwife to help me push this out. I got next (insider).

To you the reader of this book, I pray that you will be strengthened through this. That you will not focus on the negative, but that you will see the grace and beauty that came as a result of my ashes (**Isaiah 61:3**). Whatever it is that you are going through, first please know that you are not going through alone however you are *Growing* through this. I pray that God Himself will stretch out in you and that you will be able to endure the temporary pain and reach for every promise that is spoken over your life. It is time for us to take back what the enemy thought he stole (our minds, our peace). I often say that we have to be real, so that we can heal. I pray that this book does not offend you, but that it shows you that you are not alone in your struggles. Let's take back our rightful positions, you are more than a conqueror – We are given one life to live, Do not leave anything on the table!

The Forward

This is a Story of Hope. This is my story.

As Kingdom Citizens, I like to think that we are all half-breeds. The Bible says we are to be "in the world, but not of it" (John 17:16). Therefore we are half carnal, half spirit. We are all born into this world that we so desperately try to fit into - a world that we were never originally designed to fit into. This world is not our home, but we are merely planted here.

My hometown Mayodan, North Carolina was given its name for being the place where the Mayo & Dan rivers meet. Throughout this book, you will notice Lotus flowers. Lotus flowers grow directly out of muddy and murky waters yet somehow produce beautiful white blossoms.

Like the Lotus Flower,
We too have the ability to Rise from the mud
Bloom out of the darkness and Radiate into the world.
Unknown Author

In general this flower exudes much beauty and grace despite of where it began - It still blooms.

Wherever your 'here' began and wherever your 'here' has taken and continues to take you, you are planted here with a purpose! It may have taken some time for me to figure out, but now I know without a doubt that I was created to stand out, no matter what crowd I am in even though I so desperately wanted to just blend in. He created me and you to reach up, stand out, and bloom. Whatever your story is, it is for God's Glory. Just bloom!

CHAPTER 1:

Misplaced Confidence < In•Security

In the late 70's, my mother (who is white) and my father (who is black) fell in love, real love. They fell for each other hard and fast. They were high school sweethearts in a time and place that did not find their love so sweet solely because the colors of their skin did not match. When my grandparents (my mom's parents) found out, my grandfather told my mother that if she ever brought him home that he would shoot him, and this was not mere lip service. If my grandfather were alive today; I am pretty sure that he would be adorning a red MAGA hat. Despite the warnings, my parents were in love and they persisted to sneak around to see each other. Right after high school, my dad went into the military and my mom ran away with him to marry him with just a few personal belongings in their car and a whole lot of love for each other. Once they were married, they were trying so desperately to have me. They were in love and really wanted to have a baby together. My mom told me they tried several times and that she even saw a doctor to make sure she could bear a child; their prayers were finally answered when she became pregnant with me. This has always blessed me to know how much love they had for each other and how desperately they were trying to have me. I was conceived in love and *In Security*. It is so refreshing to know how much they wanted me even though this world would later not accept me.

Growing up in the small town of Mayodan, North Carolina as one of the only bi-racial girls in my age group in the 80's-90's, I struggled with so many insecurities. I am realizing now that we all have them, especially us women; It seems as though we are born with them. Now that I am a "girl mom" myself, I am reminded of what it is like to be a little girl. My seven-year-old daughter has them. I had them and still find myself overcoming them at times. No matter how much my mother affirmed me and told me I was beautiful, it still was not enough. Insecurity causes us to take our confidence off of God and place it in our doubts and fears. From little girls to grown women, we all have them. Even the most confident woman you can think of in your mind battles them. I recently asked myself "why", only to discover that the answer dates all the way back to the beginning of creation. In the book of Genesis, when the serpent approached Eve, he used insecurity to throw her off track. He asked her "Did God really say that? Did God really say to do that?", and that is exactly how insecurity continues to battle us today with attempts to misplace our confidence.

Fast forward to May 2016 - I went back to Mayodan, North Carolina the very place where my insecurities were birthed, but this time it was a little different. God called me back to this same place, in His security and love to take back what the enemy thought he stole from me (my confidence). Loving You Back to Life Women's Ministry was birthed here. It was (and still is) a movement given to me by God to help restore His love back to his women there. I ministered the message out of Psalms that we *are* *fearfully* and *wonderfully* made in His image in the very place that tried to tell me differently. (Psalm 139:14, Genesis 1:27). I ministered from what was once a hurtful and broken place transformed by God to a healed place that "even in our insecurities, we are In Security", but this transformation did not take place overnight. Today I am a wife, mom of four, pastor, and entrepreneur but before any of this, I was broken.

Even in our insecurities, we are In Security

Look at the word IN-SECURE. We have come to know this as "not having or without security", but it is all about perspective. Look at it this way - even in our insecurities, we can trust that God is with us or that we are *in – Security*. Just how the serpent came to steal Eve's security, what are some areas that keep you isolated in the darkness of your insecurities and locked up in your own mind?

In order for you to break out of this pattern, I am going to ask you to write down the three biggest lies of insecurity that you tell yourself about you

1. _____

2. _____

3. _____

CHAPTER 2:

A Mother's Love

Unfortunately, before I was even walking, my parents' marriage did not work out, so my mother and I returned to her hometown. We literally had no place to go; most of her own family turned their backs on us. My Great-Grandmothers Katherine & Lillie were the ones who took us in. A couple of her siblings came along side to help her later on. As a result of being in an interracial marriage that her family did not agree on, my mom suffered a lot of rejection. Now she is here as a divorced single mother with a black baby in a time and place where this was not welcomed with open arms. Growing up, I never realized how much rejection and pain she felt during those times. She always loved me to the best that she could. She definitely made up for the love I did not receive from others. I was never close with my maternal grandparents and that was just my normal. I did not even realize that this was a thing until later on, and I know that this was as a result of my mother's love.

Her love covered up for a lot that was missing. We grew up poor as she was starting over,

but I never saw it this way. My dad remained in the
military and lived hours away, so he was not around
often when I was younger. I was so used to my
mother that even when he would come and get me, I
would miss my mom so much and cry to go back
home. I spent some time with some of my dad's
family especially when he would come into town.
but, it was basically just me and my mom for years.
My mom worked second shift to take care of us so
she could be home with me during the day. After
staying with the few family members who took us in,
and going through a few bad places she could
afford, we eventually found a good place of our
own to call home on Washington Street in Mayodan.
She stayed home to raise me until I started school.
Even though we were on welfare, I remember being
such a happy child. Being her only child, I always
had the floor with her. We were always reading,
singing little educational songs, and I absolutely
loved to play outside. We had a great yard to play
in and I used to be able to ride my bike all over the
place during that time. We may not have had a lot
of money, but she always made sure that I had what
she did not have as a kid, yet the best thing she
ever gave me was her love.

My mom introduced me to Jesus at an early age. We attended a lively Pentecostal church and a spirit filled non-denominational church. She began serving in the nursery at church and discovered Teaching as one of her gifts. She later went on to receive her Associates Degree in Early Childhood Development. When I was around eight or nine, I vividly remember seeing my mom get baptized in a river. She was filled with the Holy Spirit and began speaking in tongues or what I later learned was her heavenly language. I was baptized shortly after.

As a child, I was often sick with ear or throat issues. The enemy tried to cancel my hearing and my voice early on - but God. I experienced my very first God encounter as a result. I kept having to be treated for ear infections, so my doctor set an appointment for a specialist to put tubes in my ears on the following Monday. I remember going to the non -denominational church with my mom the Sunday before and during an altar call. I clearly remember asking my mom could Jesus heal my ears. She told me yes, but I had to believe. She asked me if I believed He could, and I said "yes". She took me to the altar. Brother Fred laid his hands on my ears and prayed over them. I remember raising my hands

19

to God in that moment and believing. I remember my mom being blessed so much by this moment too. I cannot say that anything special happened to the natural eye, but the next morning we went to the specialist at 8a.m. We went in, he checked my ears and said "Her ears are all clear! There's nothing for me to do" We left out in, what had to be five minutes; I remember us both giving God all the glory.

This was the day I first believed,

and it was a very good day!

CHAPTER 3:

"Mixed Messages"

"a showing of thoughts or feelings that are very different from each other,"

In 1990, Mariah Carey released her video for the song entitled "Someday". I was ten years old at the time and this video was monumental for me. This was the first time I had ever seen anyone who looked remotely like me on television. It was like she had written this song and created this video just for me.

After my parents divorced and my mom returned home, her family eventually came around. As I was growing up in my earlier years, I was mostly around my mother and her family. Once I started school, I attempted to have mainly white friends because that is what I was used to being around. There were not many actresses, models, or even dolls that looked like me at the time. The closest doll that resembled me during that time was Barbie's friend, Theresa. As a result, everything that I associated beauty and/or popularity with at that time was white. Once I began school, I was quickly reminded that I was different.

Rejection

In elementary school, my skin was much darker because I loved to play outside, so when I was asked why my skin was so dark more than once, it made me feel like I was damaged goods. I recall the times when little white boys I had huge crushes on would tell me, "my mom said I can't like you because your dad is black" or times when my white grandmother would say passive aggressive things to me like, "are you going to wear your hair like that?" These were all very confusing things for me to encounter as a child. When I would lose friends as a result of having a black dad, I chose to lie and tell them that I was Native American instead, since that seemed more accepting at the time; when I would tell them the truth, I would still lose them. I was a misfit. I was called half-breed, mixed, skunk, zebra, nigger, grey baby, the list goes on. Several times I was asked the most ignorant questions like, If I had a choice which race would I rather be or silly statements like, "You are so lucky you get to date both."

22

These all sent messages to my inner self that I was broken or just a little "off" and that I would never measure up. When I was around fifteen years old, my step-mother (who is also white) told me something about my childhood that shook me to my core; she told me that when I was very little I stayed over with them one night, and she caught me in the bathtub scrubbing my skin vigorously. She told me that she asked me what I was doing and that I responded that I "wanted to be white like her and my mommy". This breaks me down to write this even now to know that that is what life's messages sent to me at such an early age. I had a handful of friends throughout elementary school who came and went and to make things worse, I started my menstrual cycle early in the fourth grade. It was extremely heavy and never ending. It was so bad that I had to be put on medication to stop it and try to reset it. This further intensified things for me and alienated me as a young girl.

Heaven Sent Friend
In the fifth grade, God sent me an angel (Rest in Heaven Kristen Elizabeth Sutphin) who quickly became my best friend. She was way out of my league in my opinion. She lived in the Country

Club near Madison and somehow she befriended little ol' me. We would spend the night with each other, she would go on trips with me, and she taught me a lot. She took me to the Country Club with her (yes there is a Country Club right outside of Madison), we would swim together, she taught me how to play tennis, and I even joined the school tennis team with her, but honestly, I always felt out of place around others with her. She never once made me feel that way, but deep inside I felt like I did not measure up. Other people would remind us of my difference, and she would get fighting mad with them. She was such an angel on earth that God decided to take her at an early age right after high school graduation. I am so grateful for the purpose she fulfilled in my life during that small window we had. Our friendship was during a time where I was trying to find my place and find love and acceptance. Her friendship opened me up to a whole new world and it helped pull me out of one of the biggest pits of my life.

Me too

We became friends around the time that childhood molestation was happening to me. Prior to this, I found myself in a sexual relationship with a female relative for over a year. No one person could ever understand the pain of rejection, the shame, the loneliness that I hid behind my smile for years. I suffered many years in silence from the guilt and shame of childhood molestation of which I clung to; it was the one thing in my life (at the time) that resembled anything like acceptance, so this proceeded for a long time. Honestly I enjoyed it, and I would cry when I was not able to go to her house. Again after years of being told I was not enough, this somehow made me feel that I was enough for the moment. She was older than me and was exploring her own sexuality at my expense. It all came to a sudden stop once she was in high school and got her first boyfriend, which left me with even more rejection and even more lost and confused than before. As a matter of fact, I never even categorized this as sexual abuse or molestation until years later in my twenties once God revealed it to me and my healing process began. Hurt, shame, and guilt told me to suppress it and never speak on it. I was absolutely convinced that this was on me, that it was somehow my fault, and that it was somehow my fault again when it stopped. It was not until God woke me up one morning and had me look up the word 'molestation' in the dictionary.

According to The Legal Dictionary, the legal definition of molestation is:

"the crime of sexual acts with children up to the age of 18, including touching of private parts, exposure of genitalia, taking of pornographic pictures, rape, inducement of sexual acts with the molester."

Cornell Law states that molestation also applies to "incest by a relative with a minor family member and any unwanted sexual acts with adults short of rape."

The thing is, as a victim of sexual abuse, you never asked to be touched in that way. Regardless of how you responded or reacted to it, it was still sexual abuse.

Everyone's healing process is different. Sometimes God can and will heal you immediately and other times, healing can be a process. For me, there were several layers to this word molestation. He showed me that one of the very first seeds ever planted from this was when I was in early elementary school during carpet time. There was a (white) boy that sat beside me and would put his hand down the back of my pants where no one else could see. As a result of the root of rejection and me craving acceptance, I would always try to sit beside him so this would occur. This went on a few times until one day I noticed him sitting beside another little white girl and I saw him do it to her. It crushed me and that is where the seeds of rejection and molestation grew from. Most recently, God revealed things going too far with one of my half-brothers at my dad's house during the first molestation. I was playing house with two of my brothers and something so innocent took a turn. Something that I started went too far was the message that I received. I remember wanting to play "house" and wanting to play "mommy and daddy". I allowed one of my brothers to get on top of me, but then it went too far. I recall vividly as he slid my shorts to the side, he did not penetrate me through my underwear, but I remember hating him once it happened. I again was convinced that this was my fault and that I allowed this. I am pretty sure this is why I was never comfortable around him afterwards and stopped going to my dad's house for a while even though he did not live there. Shame told me to never speak of it, and that my dad would somehow love me less, so I buried it and it has remained suppressed until now.

I was deceived to believe that since I willingly participated in these acts that none of this was classified as molestation much less sexual abuse until God showed me differently and that at the very root of it all was rejection. Once it ceased, it made things even worse for me. At the point when it all ended with the female, I was still a virgin, but it awakened sexual perversion inside of me.

No one person could ever understand the pain of rejection, the shame, the loneliness that I hid behind my smile for years.

Pause & Reflect

I know this may have been a lot for you to handle at one time. Healing is a process. Like me, maybe you have subconsciously suppressed certain acts that could be the very root that is vital to your healing. **After reading this, is there anything that God is revealing to you in this area? Take a minute and write out your thoughts/feelings/prayers here:**

_____

_____

_____

From one extreme to another

Shortly after this, my middle school years began, and I started to embrace my "black side". Black boys were definitely not ashamed of me, matter of fact they seemed to want to parade me around like some sort of award-winning pony, completely opposite of before when white boys liked me in secret; it was like going from one extreme to the other. However, most black girls quickly made me feel like I was too much yet not enough at the same time and that my skin, which was once too dark for others, was too light for them and that my hair which was too unruly for others is now too "good" for them as if having this skin and hair somehow made me and my life perfect; when actually it did the opposite. I was never fully accepted as black only merely tolerated for being half black or mixed. I was too dark for one part of me and too light for the other at the same time. It made me different, which ultimately translated into tons of rejection when all I desperately wanted was to be loved and accepted.

In the sixth grade, I met my very first friend who was mixed like me then Kristen and I drifted apart as middle school continued. For the first time ever, I felt like someone could finally understand me (all sides of me), but honestly, we were both a little wild and things quickly spun further out of control for me. Unfortunately, the teacher's salary did not work out for my mother, so she worked hard in the textile industry. She was working a second shift job to provide for us, and I was a latch-key kid. I would come home from school and she would be at work until after midnight. She worked this shift to make more money for us. Nevertheless, she began seeing a co-worker and over time this new relationship ended up being bad. We had already left the home that I grew up in in Mayodan and we ended up living with him; this is when things went from bad to worse. The person she loved so dearly did not love himself very much. He was an alcoholic and one night he drank too much which resulted in domestic abuse; I will never forget this night. I was awakened from sleep to hear the two of them arguing. The next thing I knew, my mom came in to get me and her head was bleeding. We ran next door to the neighbor's house for safety, but we eventually went back soon after. These were dark times for me as I was trying to process all of this; all of these things happened to me by the age of twelve.

I remember one night I decided I was going to end it all. We were living in the man's trailer, and I was home alone doing math homework. Suicidal thoughts became rampant as I convinced myself that things would be better if I would just end it all right there. I found my mom's nerve pills, swallowed a handful, finished my homework, and woke up the next morning! I woke up confused yet convinced at the same time that God was not through with me yet. Even in the midst of all this hurt and confusion, I still knew God's voice from earlier in my childhood. Both of my parents told me that God showed them that there was a calling on my life. My paternal Great Grandmother Katherine once told me that I have the spiritual gift of healing (which took me years to figure out that not only is there such a thing as physical healing but mental and spiritual healing as well.) These things were all good things yet still confusing amongst the mixed messages in my mind.

It was like I went from one extreme to the next. During elementary school, I wanted to be white so bad that I had full on 80's hair with the big bangs and wore preppy styled clothes. Remember the scrunchies, pegged jeans, and slouch socks? Yes, that was me! In middle school, I tried so hard to be black. I fully embraced the culture and rocked all the 90's black hairstyles from French rolls to finger waves (shout out to my aunt Puddy for keeping my hair tight back then). I wore baggy clothes and my sneaker game was real strong.

Deep down I was desperately searching for my identity and trying to find my place. No one person could fully understand.

Being the only child with my mom, I recall always wanting to be the center of attention but at this point I no longer wanted to be seen. I dimmed my once shining light a lot around others for years especially in crowds; only those closest to me would see the real me shine through. All I wanted to do was blend in, but little did I know God created me to stand out. This took years for me to decipher through all the messages from others and mostly myself. At times, I still have to be reminded that it is okay for me to be my true self. I know now that I will never be white enough or black enough (nor do I have to be); I am simply *me* and that is more than enough and that I, like you, have been *fearfully and wonderfully made and created in the image of*

God (Psalm 139:14 & Genesis 1:27). We had no say in how we were created. God Himself took the time out to intricately design each and every one of us differently for His purpose to be fulfilled in the earth. *How marvelous are His Works?!*

Self-Reflection

How does it make you feel to hear that God took
the time out to create you - the way you look, think,
where you live, even how you speak?
To know that God created you just the way you are,
and He calls you Beautiful — flaws and all?

_____

_____

_____

_____

_____

❁

You formed my innermost being, shaping my
delicate inside
and my intricate outside,
and wove them all together in my mother's
womb.
14 I thank you, God, for making me so
mysteriously complex!
Everything you do is marvelously breathtaking.
It simply amazes me to think about it!
How thoroughly you know me, Lord!
15 You even formed every bone in my body

when you created me in the secret place,
carefully, skillfully shaping me from nothing to
something.
¹⁶ You saw who you created me to be before I
became me!
Before I'd ever seen the light of day,
the number of days you planned for me
were already recorded in your book.
^{17–18} Every single moment you are thinking of me!
How precious and wonderful to consider
that you cherish me constantly in your every
thought!
O God, your desires toward me are more
than the grains of sand on every shore!
When I awake each morning, you're still with me.

Psalm 139:13-17/18

The Passion Translation

Think About It!

The Dangers of Comparison

Why do we worry so much about the exterior things
more than the interior?
Our skin, hair, nails - these are all temporary.

We are more concerned with how we present
ourselves to others more than we are concerned
about how we present ourselves to God.
*Remember man looks at the outer appearance God
sees the heart (or intent). 1 Samuel 16:7*

**"Charm can be misleading, and beauty is vain
and so quickly fades, but this virtuous woman
lives in the wonder, awe, and fear of the Lord.
She will be praised throughout eternity. So go
ahead and give her the credit that is due, for she
has become a radiant woman, and all her loving
works of righteousness deserve to be admired at
the gateways of every city!"
Proverbs 31:30-31 TPT**

A flower does not think of competing

with the flower next to it. It just blooms. – Zen Chin

CHAPTER 4

Miss Understood

Thanksgiving 1992, my mom purchased her first home in Madison, North Carolina. Our home was built from the ground up, so we were able to watch it in all stages from the foundation to completion. These were exciting times for us; I did not realize at the time what a huge accomplishment this was for her, a single mom with a half black child at the age of thirty-two, purchasing her own home. Wow, my mom was overcoming so many barriers and opposition in spite of what people thought of her and without the support of others! I am realizing more and more that she taught me so much without even articulating this - her actions spoke louder than words. At the time, I honestly thought that this house would somehow be the answer to my prayers and that she would leave this man once and for all, but that was not the case. He eventually moved in with us after convincing my mom that he would stop drinking, but that eventually took a downward spiral.

As a result of the recent molestations, all the newfound attention from boys and hanging with a new crowd, I quickly spun further out of control. When I was twelve, my doctor put me on birth control to regulate my menstrual cycle. I used this and my mom's work schedule to my advantage. I started drinking alcohol and smoking marijuana with my friends which ultimately led to me having sex when I was just thirteen years old. Not just one time either. I was having sex with multiple partners. It was like I kept going and going and going like the Energizer Bunny. I was much like how a woman would describe a man as a "Player" - I would use a man for what he had and then move on to the next one. It was as if this somehow made up for what had happened to me. This made me feel like I was in control, and these became the methods I used to numb my pain. I chose these methods to self-medicate. I put up walls and would not allow anyone in. Every day it was like I would have to wake up and repeat the same vicious cycle to keep all these feelings suppressed and for me to stay numb. This went on for quite some time, and I am sure that my wild ways were also putting a strain on my mom's relationship with her boyfriend. One night I was at home during one of their altercations. They were arguing and I had heard enough, so I decided to put an end to it. I went out of my room and I fought this grown man. I got called a "nigger lover" and was asked why I was doing *this* to my mother. How could me being part of who I am hurt my mother? Side note: I am in no way saying this was how she felt or that any of this was her fault. Again, my mother loved me this I know, yet I believe she received mixed messages of her own that she was broken and/or damaged goods for being with a black man and having a black child. I know now that her being in this particular relationship was a direct result of her own rejection; however the longer she stayed in this relationship, the further it pushed me away from her at the time.

Every day I would wake up and repeat the same vicious cycle to keep all these feelings suppressed to stay numb

Self-Reflection

After years of rejection, racial discrimination, domestic abuse, emotional abuse, suicidal thoughts, and addictions I chose to self-medicate prior to totally surrendering these areas to God.

Ask yourself this question -

Are there any areas in my life (past or current) where I am self-medicating and not allowing the Holy Spirit to fill me completely in?

_____

_____

_____

_____

_____

_____

_____

_____

_____

_____

Prayer

Father, I ask that you show me, me. If there are any areas that I am not allowing you to completely fill, I pray that you reveal them to me. Not for me to condemn myself, but for me to release to you. Father allow me to give myself grace and patience as you begin to show me these things, so that I can be healed and Set Free in Jesus Name. Amen.

CHAPTER 5

Perfection is the Enemy

As a child, I was only used to being around my mom. My dad remained in the military, remarried, had more kids, and was stationed in Fayetteville, North Carolina which was hours away from me. I would see him from time to time, especially for family reunions, but honestly I do not remember him being in my life in my early years as much as I do in my later years. I know this was also as a result of when I would go to his house; I would miss my mom so much and cry to go home. I am sure that had an effect on him as well. I used to love for him to come to town and take me to see family. We would spend time at my late Papa Vernon's (aka Big Jim) and my late Great Grandma Katherine's. I loved seeing all of my beautiful aunts, uncles, and cousins. But honestly, I did not go around them as often as I should have when my dad was not around because it made me miss him too much.

Around '93- '94, my dad and I began to get closer, but this was also around the same time that he was being re-stationed to Germany. Him leaving me to go to Germany was hard and seemed like right when we got closer, he had to go. This hurt and I continued on my downtrodden path of self-destruction. Once I got to high school, I was still living my life of self-medication. I was still trying to find my place. I seemed to have a few friends but not any real true friends outside of who I considered my best friend, but we were not in the same school district anymore. I did have one girl who I considered to be close with or at least as close as I would allow one to get. One night after a football game, I was with a guy at McDonalds; this is where we would all come to hang out after games in our small town. I was jumped by three girls over this guy and found out that "my friends" watched from the other parking lot. Prior to this, I had never been in an actual fight before other than with my mom's boyfriend. I was furious because I never would have fought a girl over a guy then. We were not that serious because I was not even looking for that. The girls who jumped me were black girls. After the fight was broken up, I recall so clearly the guy asking me what I wanted to do. I wanted revenge! I wanted to fight her fair and square because this was not right. He took me to where they were and just as I was about to get out the car, my cousin Christina comes jumping out of a moving car screaming "Jump on her

46

now". I spent time with "Christine" at my Great Grandmother Katherine's house. Christine accepted me and loved me because I was family (and even though we do not talk or see each other as much now I know she still does). Her coming to fight for me in that moment was so monumental for me in a time when I felt so alone, even though I was with this guy. No one person could understand the rage and loneliness I was feeling.   I was like a ticking time bomb ready to implode! I say implode because to everyone on the outside they saw perfection, but inside there was such an internal conflict.

At the time my hair was long so the girl who jumped me pulled my hair and scratched me. So right after the fight, I cut my hair to make sure that this would never happen again. If someone wanted to fight me again they would have to fight me, and not just pull my hair. I also believe I did it to fit in and make others comfortable. I would try to lay low and not bring any additional attention to myself since my physical appearance seemed to be a problem and had caused so much jealousy before.

I even went through a period of secretly cutting myself. I hated the skin I was in and people had no clue. This attack was basically the straw that broke the camel's back for me. It made me so angry,

47

because all she had to do was tell me to leave him alone and that is what I would have done. I was not out here trying to take girls' boyfriends. I was simply trying to cope; not making excuses for my behavior, but again, this was my self-medication. If you are reading this and I have ever hurt you as a result of this, please forgive me as I have forgiven me. But I wore men like garments at the time. I would put them on and take them off just like that. They were disposable to me.

That summer I obtained my worker's permit and got my first job to try to focus my sights on to something else. The main source of employment in Madison-Mayodan is the textile industry. Most people there have worked hard in this industry for most of their lives. My mom tirelessly worked in this industry to provide for us and I am grateful, but it only took one summer job working in this field for me to quickly realize this is not what I wanted for myself.

My dad and I were talking more on the regular and my mom wanted me to have him in my life especially since I was out of control by this time. Like any good mother would, she ended up switching companies and took a first shift job to be home with me since I was doing things I should not be doing

48

during her second shift. This also caused a power struggle for me since I was so used to doing what I wanted. I was sneaking out at night and would come and go as I pleased. After many heated discussions with her, we decided I would go stay with my dad. She was desperate for me to be happy and wanted what was best for me. So in August 1995, the beginning of my sophomore year of High School, I boarded a plane to go live with my dad in Germany with the idea of never returning to Madison-Mayodan, North Carolina ever again. I was fifteen years old and had never been on a plane before. I flew fourteen hours alone desperate for something bigger and/or better than what Madison had ever offered me. I had only traveled a few places outside of North Carolina with my mom prior to this. Matter of fact, I had never been away from her for more than a week before this, but now here I am moving away from her to a whole other country. I felt it was the right thing for me to do and that it was the best decision for us both. I wanted her and her boyfriend to be happy and if that meant me leaving then that is what I would do, but little did I know that this separation would be one of the hardest things we would encounter.

Perfection and Performance

When I moved in with my dad at the end of that summer, I went from being the only child to being the oldest child. This taught me responsibility and how to work with others. We were a blended family and my stepmom sowed seeds into me that I would later use when I became a Bonus Mom. When I was with my dad, I somehow convinced myself as a child that he went on and made a perfect family without me, so I wanted to be the perfect daughter for him. Although I was far from perfect, I still strived to be that for him. I became a people pleaser as a result of all the rejection (especially when it came to my dad) thinking that if I looked perfect and did everything perfectly, perhaps they would not leave me.

For the first year, everything was perfect. We did things together as a family that I had never experienced before like family meetings, camping, and repelling off a mountain. I went to an American military school and for the first time in my life, I became one of MANY half-breeds. There were mixtures from all over the world. I was far from little old Mayodan, North Carolina. My dad was military so there were always rules to abide by, but as long as I did my part I was able to do things that I

50

wanted to do. God gifted me with wisdom, and my parents always trusted me (more importantly God) to do what was right. They allowed me freedom to make my own mistakes, but at the same time would reel me back in when necessary. I was able to experience European club life and I honestly experienced a little too much "life" with some of my new friends and some soldiers there. I was having the time of my life y'all. My first summer break came, and I went back home to visit my mom. She was doing so much better after dealing with me leaving and had left the guy. I know now that God had His hands on her. It was hard for us to depart a second time, but we trusted God.

I adjusted to my new life; another school year quickly went by and I visited home again the following summer. This time I reconnected with someone very important in my life. I met Bryan Lowe for the first time (in person) in the summer of '97. The funny thing is we had been "Phone Buddies" for years prior to this and never actually met in person until then. We were friends first. We would spend hours on the phone being carefree, laughing, and singing as friends. There was something about him that was pretty undeniable once we met and connected that summer. We fell for each other hard and fast. It is funny how one summer can change everything. Summer break was coming to an end and I had to make a decision. I was torn about staying home then. After much contemplation, I decided to return to Germany. I felt it was the right thing for me to do at the time. Plus things were finally starting to look up for me, but then my life took quite a turn once I returned back to Germany.

Imperfection

I ended up getting very close with my stepmom during my stay. She created a monster and turned me into a girly girl. I was able to completely come out of my shell here. I discovered a love for dresses, heels, and purses through her. We were so close that people would not believe we were not actual mother and daughter. We all started going to church together as a family. My dad introduced me to praise and worship. He would take my siblings and I to various places to sing. Due to my dad getting a sports injury and being confined for a while, we slowly stopped going to church together then infidelity crept in (all the enemy needs is a small entrance) and my dad and stepmom eventually separated. Honestly, this destroyed me all over again. I was not old enough to personally experience the effects from when my parents divorced so this was truly detrimental to me. My seventeen-year-old self could not understand how you could be married for sixteen years and then POOF it all ends just like that. I thought if this is what love and marriage looks like, then I definitely did not want any parts of it. My stepmom and my siblings ended up moving back to the states. I stayed with my dad and his new pregnant girlfriend who was not that much older than me. I was left feeling hurt, angry, and even more confused. My dad was in a new position in the military and was stationed in the field more, so I was home alone with her.

Now my dad provided for me and made sure I was financially secure, but this abrupt transition resurfaced a lot of things in me. I was far from emotionally secure. This pushed me further into my self-numbing devices, partying, staying out late, and/or not coming home for days. I was trying to hang on to the voice of God in my life, but at this point Daddy's Girl was hurt. The following school year, I returned back home even more broken than before. When I left this place, my dad and I were no longer speaking, and I vowed to never get married and never have kids (and I am sure God laughed at this vow).

Good Father

The funny thing is that when I thought I was running from God all the way to Germany I ended up running head-first into Him. I met a lady there who prophesied to me about the soon to be separation before it even happened. God prepared me for it, but it still hurt. I thought I was going to Germany to build a relationship with my Dad which I did, but I ended up getting to know My Heavenly Father even more. I know now that this had to happen because I needed to know that my dad was not perfect. I also needed this to learn that God is perfect, and He does not want us to perform for Him. His love never quits, and His grace is so sufficient for us and that is all we need. The bible says in 1 Samuel 16:7 that man looks at the outer appearance, but God looks at the heart (or the intent). People judge things based on performance. Anytime you mention how something, or someone works or performs, you are talking about their performance. Rejection and Performance work together with Perfection. They tell you the more you perform, the more you will be accepted or granted

54

access to something, yet God tells us that the only thing that we should work (or perform) towards is entering his place of Rest. (Hebrews 4:11) Perfection is our enemy. We do not have to be perfect because of God's Perfect Love oh and His Grace!

No one person could understand the rage and loneliness I was feeling. Everyone on the outside saw perfection, but inside there was such an internal conflict

Think About It

God is Perfect and He does not want us to perform for Him. Rejection and Performance work together with Perfection. Perfection is our enemy.
Ask yourself this question:

Are there currently any areas where I am performing for certain individuals in my life instead of just being who God has called me to be?

_____

_____

_____

_____

_____

_____

_____

_____

_____

_____

Word of Wisdom

The walls we use to protect ourselves are the same walls

that imprison us with our pain

and keep us from getting closer to God.

I am no stranger to rejection, and neither is God.

We can be vulnerable.

Mirror Time

It is okay to be vulnerable especially with God. He longs for these moments with us. Take this time out and find a mirror. Look into the mirror and really ask yourself why you do the things that you do. Is it because you are chasing love and acceptance or things beyond what God originally created you to be? Are you so busy striving for acceptance when God Himself called you before time began? What did not kill you only made you stronger because God broke through. We see ourselves through tainted lenses from what has happened to us in the past, but God our Creator looks at us in all TRUTH. Listen — people are full of opinions, God is full of Truth. I have been called a lot of different things, but most importantly I now understand that I am called and that supersedes it all. Do you not know that long before you made your first mistake, your first failure, He had already called you and set you apart? I pray that today you start to see the reflection staring back at you in the mirror as Beautifully Loved and Accepted. **Say it with me:**

"I am Beautifully Loved and Accepted!"

CHAPTER 6

Miss Independent

Once I returned back home to Madison after being exposed to a different culture, my mindset had completely changed. I still hated my school experiences there and I made up in my mind that I was not going back to school there. I vowed again that I would not go back there so my mom agreed to let me move with my best friend and her mom to Wilmington, N.C.; this lasted all of three months before I ended up right back home with my mom. Things were not working out between my friend and me. My mom had to come and take me to the doctor where I was diagnosed with an STD and it was during this time, that the doctor told me I would never be able to bare children in which this further pushed me against the idea of marriage and having kids. This also broke me down and forced me to recognize it was time to let it go and go back home with my mom but letting go was not that easy.

After returning home a second time, my pride said I will just quit school before I go back to school there. It was now my senior year, but I was determined that I would not go back to high school there, so I took the GED test. Once I finished the exams, the lady went over my scores with me. She looked at me and prophetically said "Baby, you don't belong here". Boy was she right in so many ways. This resonated within me, so I swallowed my pride and went back to complete my senior year in Madison, North Carolina.

I reunited with my now husband during this time, but he had no clue what he was getting himself into and little did we know that God had set things in motion for us at the time. I was so hurt by my previous encounters, but I fused it into anger because that felt much better than hurt. I thought I was more in control with anger versus being hurt and vulnerable, so I closed myself off as a defense mechanism. My now husband loved me so much that he followed me all the way to Wilmington, N.C. to visit me when I lived there. It was still hard for me to receive it. In fact, it took him getting locked up (which is part of his testimony) for me to tell him I love him for the first time, but God used his love to help heal me. Bryan Lowe eventually wore me down; the love God placed in his heart for me was and still is undeniable. He saw me and he loves me for me. We have been through a lot together as we have both grown up together. We have had some ups, but we experienced a lot of downs trying to figure life out. Prior to my graduation, he took me to my senior prom. This was a miracle within itself being that he was on intense probation at the time (again part of his story). We were young and we loved each other, but there was still some learning to love that we needed to do.

Fear of Commitment

Generational curses are real. My paternal grandfather had twenty-eight kids all by different women (yes, you read that right). After all that I had endured up until this point, I honestly did not know how to just be with one partner. Bryan and I both came with baggage, and I was afraid of commitment.

Side Note: Fear of commitment or Commitment Phobia is real. According to PsychCentral, Common causes of commitment phobia may include:

- Fear of, or having had, the relationship end without notice or signs
- Fear of not being in the "right" relationship

- Fear of, or having been in, an unhealthy relationship (characterized by abandonment, infidelity, abuse, etc.)
- Trust issues because of past hurts by those close to the person
- Childhood trauma or abuse
- Unmet childhood needs or attachment issues
- Complicated family dynamics while growing up

I had experienced just about all of these. Right after graduation, God blessed me with a good job. It came during a time when I was searching for something greater. Through this, I was able to relocate to The Triad and get my own place the day before my nineteenth birthday. Bryan Lowe was not having me out here living the single life by myself, so we ultimately moved in with each other. Bryan and I eventually went on learning how to live with each other (we were both raised as the only-child), raise his son part time, have our first son (the curse breaker — in spite of what the doctor said), then marry all by the time I was 22 but I was still broken and trust me our lives were far from perfect.

Prior to this, I met my bonus son when he was just two years old and I fell in love with him. Bryan and his mother had him before our summer love story began, so there was never any animosity there for me. We had an instant connection. My stepmom already sowed seeds of love into me previously and showed me how to love unconditionally, so it was easy for me to love him. I also believed I would not have kids, so I dove head-first into loving on him and I wanted to make sure that Bryan had space and opportunity to be ever present in his life, however, I believe my love for him was misread. Things were not easy with his mother in the earlier years as we navigated through being able to see him and while Bryan learned to establish boundaries with her. Things seemed to have intensified once I had my son. It was hurtful, but I pressed on being the Independent woman I was.

I worked full time and had a great paying job. I now had a husband and my first-born son, but I was still hooked on marijuana as my self-medication. Our house was the party house on nights and weekends. There were always people around, yet I still felt alone. There was still a deep longing in my soul that could not be filled. I wanted to be better especially for my son. A few years after having him and a whole lot of life later, I accepted an invitation to church from a coworker and my life changed drastically. Two of my coworkers operated in the prophetic (of course) and God used them mightily in our life at the time. In February 2004, I re-dedicated my life back to the Lord and was saved for real. I consider February as "Love Month" and it has nothing to do with Valentine's Day. It is when I began my Love Walk with God. This is when I allowed Him to begin to (not just love me) but to lavishly pour His love on me (1 John 3:1). See people before had said they loved me and they hurt me, but I immediately came to know that this love was something different.

Look with wonder at the depth of the Father's marvelous love that he has lavished on us! He has called us and made us his very own *beloved* children.
1 John 3:1 (TPV)

Deliverance

God did a quick work in my home; I was delivered from marijuana and my husband was saved and delivered the following month! I always knew there was a calling on my life, as I was younger and called myself running from God. It was like I was saying, "Not yet God", and He allowed it because He knew the bigger picture, but I still had patterns to unlearn. I had always loved the Lord, I just did not know the proper way to love Him. It is extremely hard to love God or anybody else when you do not love or value yourself. It took the love of God to draw me in and to keep me. Even more so than me going to church, it took me seeking a personal relationship with Him and allowing Him to totally heal me. I had to make the choice to serve Him wholeheartedly no matter the cost and allow him to work on me. The fact that my kids are all by the same man who is my husband today is a true testament to God. When we got married in November 2001 people said we would not last seven days; today we are going on nineteen years of marriage. "No one can separate what God puts together" (Matthew 19:6) not even me. I had to overcome my issues that resulted from relational pain and trauma that was buried.

See Little Miss Independent chose to bury it all and I took everything on by myself even though I never really had to.

God has to reveal the trauma from our life so we can be healed, totally healed not just buried.

I am not a single mom, but in many ways I treated life with this mentality since I was raised by one. I mean my mom held it all the way down for the most part by herself. She took care of me, worked full time, took care of household things, bills, yard work, kept her car clean, and the list goes on. As a child, I saw her take these things upon herself head on and never fold. Then on top of this, I was very self-reliant being an only child. As women, we can carry a lot. I mean we were created to carry life within our bodies. Still I believe somewhere along the line we as women are taught to bury our emotions; to grin and bear it. We are somehow taught to suppress our true feelings, our hurts, and our disappointments with our spouses, with our kids, with God, even with ourselves! As women in this world today we are told to be strong and independent. We take on this "I can bear all mentality". As mothers, especially, we will not allow our kids to see us down because we have to be strong for them, and then once we receive salvation, we act as though we are supposed to be some sort

of Super Christian who can take on just about anything and help everybody. But let me ask you a question, *who is helping you?* What do we need a Savior for if we can bear all things?
In 1 Corinthians 13:7 we learn that it is only God-like love or Agape love that can do that.

Yet, we were quietly taught to sweep things under the rug, to not say a word, to just paint on this smile and push on. Never truly allowing God to deal with the abuse, the hurt, the trauma, the pain - Why?! Because it is buried so deep. We somehow have tricked ourselves to thinking we are over them, but the truth is you are just ignoring it.
If this is you,

God says, "It is time to be real so that you can heal!"

That does not mean that you have to share everything with someone - but you can give it to God right now. Let Him take it, He can handle it. He can handle you with your brokenness. He can handle you with your angry self. Stop beating yourself up. Remember when we are weak, He is strong! Let Him be God for You this once! We are so quick to believe God for someone else. This is your moment. Surrender is not weakness. In fact, it takes great strength to surrender to God. In our weakness, He is strongest.

God can handle your weakness. He did not make you this way for you to have to keep taking on more and more stuff alone. He created us to need Him.

It is time for Release! You have been carrying these things for years and every time somebody does something that even remotely reminds you of it, you are triggered, and you shut down.

Becoming < Un-Becoming

One of my favorite quotes says,

"And the day came when the risk to remain tight in a bud was more painful than the risk it took to blossom." - Anaïs Nin

Throughout my process, I have learned that life is not about becoming anything at all; it is more about un-Becoming everything that God never intended for you to become, so that you can be who He called you to be in the first place. Whatever has been holding you back - Let God get to the root of it, so you can let it go, and bloom.

And He has said to me, "My grace is sufficient for you, for power is perfected in weakness." Most gladly, therefore, I will rather boast about my weaknesses, so that the power of Christ may dwell in me. 10 Therefore I am well content with weaknesses, with insults, with distresses, with persecutions, with difficulties, for Christ's sake; for when I am weak, then I am strong.
2 Corinthians 12:9-10 NASB

Pause & Reflect

Be real with yourself. Be real with God. Are there certain areas where you are not allowing Him in? Are there areas where you will not fully relinquish control? Are there areas of anger that are truly hurts?

After reading this, is there anything that God is revealing to you in this area? Take a minute and write out your thoughts/feelings/prayers here.

_____

_____

_____

_____

_____

_____

_____

_____

_____

_____

My Prayer for You

God I thank you for the person reading this right
now. God I thank you that you are here with them
now and you stand ready to take on every hurt,
every burden, and every care. God strengthen the
reader right now to be able to trust you with their
most vulnerable places even now. God I thank You
that they are releasing these things to You right now
and will continue to release them to you as they
come back to remembrance. God I thank You for
loving us so much and for caring about us. I thank
You for showing us that we were never created to
do everything on our own. You created us to be who
You called us to be. I thank You that You have sent
us The Helper (Holy Spirit) to assist us when we need
it. **God I thank You for your Grace.**

CHAPTER 7
Graced for This

✿

The LORD replied, "Don't say, 'I'm too young,' for
you must go wherever I send you and say
whatever I tell you. And don't be afraid of the
people, for I will be with you and will protect you.
I, the LORD, have spoken!" Then the LORD
reached out and touched my mouth and said,

"Look, I have put my words in your mouth!
Today I appoint you to stand up
against nations and kingdoms.
Some you must uproot and tear down,
destroy and overthrow.
Others you must build up and plant."
Jeremiah 1:7-10

I have been called Jackie most of my life,
but my birth name, Jaclyn, means *supplanter: one
who uproots and then replaces with something else*
and that is exactly what God allowed. I was
allowed to be broken by people, but God

gracefully held on to me, and He is still building me back up brick by brick so that I can gracefully help build others. I have learned that God is with us in every place of our lives. We acknowledge Him most in the high places, but He is most intricately with us in the lows. It is in the low places where life seems to be breaking us that God is in fact making us, and that is where the anointing flows. As I reflect, I have spent the majority of my life surviving. As I am entering my fortieth year of life, I feel as though I owe it to myself to live more intentional – to thrive. The first twenty years of my life were crazy then the rest I have spent with God unlearning things from my past experiences even from church (which taught me more about personal relationship with God over religion).

Now it is time to thrive - no more survival mode!

What happened to me does not define me however when trauma occurs, it does alter how one responds or reacts. According to The American Counseling Association, childhood sexual abuse victims experience long term effects such as depression, guilt, shame, self-blame, eating disorders, somatic concerns (excessive thoughts, feelings and behaviors relating to physical symptoms), anxiety, dissociative patterns, repression, denial, sexual problems, and relationship problems. Does any of this sound familiar?

Regardless of what I have endured, as a result I am a very empathetic person. When I returned back to my senior year of high school, I vividly remember meeting with my guidance counselor, Ms. Capel, who very well helped me to decide to come back and finish. In deciding what I would like to become in life, all I knew was that I wanted to help people. She suggested the medical field for me, so I leaned towards becoming a physical therapist. I did not end up taking that route so to speak, but later on I did end up studying psychology and Christian Counseling. In a sense as a pastor, people come to me wounded and are in need of "spiritual therapy" to exercise on a daily basis. As Christians, we are to work out our own salvation with fear and trembling (Philippians 2:12), not "fear" as in being afraid or tormented, but instead, reverence to God. In this world, we will have trouble. We will suffer trauma. My trauma may not look like your trauma and vice versa. What happened to me (and you) does not define me (and

73

you). The past is just that, the past. I am moving forward into my true purpose pre-designed by God before I even took my first breath. Has life been perfect? No, but it is all about perspective. As I am approaching forty years old, I see things differently now. I am not the same and still evolving and growing everyday. I am a leader and as I look back now, I see a whole tribe of gracefully kept women trudging the path that has been trail blazed for them. Luke 1:45 is my Life Application Verse and says this:

"And blessed is she who believed that there would be a fulfillment of what had been spoken to her by the Lord."

I believe for me but more than that, I believe for you! No matter who you are, let's keep marching forward because we are *Graced for This*.

Today I am a founding pastor of Freedom Ministries Church & Outreach, but before any of this, I had to allow God to do the work in me. Getting saved is the easy part. My personal journey to Freedom has not been easy and it still can get lonely at times, yet I am never alone (Deuteronomy 31:6, Hebrews 13:5). I had (and must continue) to die to myself daily, so I can help guide others on their personal journeys to Freedom in Christ. When counseling others, I always seek to look at things from all different perspectives. I was given the gift of wisdom at an early age. This too was confusing to figure out at times because my parents and other adults would often talk to me about personal things and I would give advice.

Fear is a Liar

As a child, the enemy introduced me to fear at an early age. I experienced paralyzing fear at night. I would wet the bed because I was too scared to get up. I was and still am a *seer*. What is a seer? A seer is *a perceiver of hidden truth*. I have always had a keen sense of discernment. I sense things that no one else sees. I was later exposed to the spiritual realm by my uncle Jerome (my dad's brother) and his wife Angelena. I remember them coming into town when I was younger and praying that yokes would be broken off of our family, but not having any clue exactly what they meant at the time. As a result, I am no novice to deliverance and spiritual warfare. As a child, fear used to keep me bound and even into adulthood it kept me within certain limits. That yoke has since been broken off of me and every generational curse stops with me.

I am learning even as I am writing this book that we can learn to face our fears and tackle them head on. Fear is a normal human reaction to something that is bigger than you but know this we do not have to take up residency in fear. It has been said that the Bible tells us to "Fear Not" 366 times. That covers every day of the year plus the extra day for leap year. That is powerful!
God knew we would struggle with fear and He has already equipped us with His Word (366 times to be exact) and His Spirit to tackle things beyond our control and our comfort levels.

"For God will never give you the spirit of fear, but the Holy Spirit who gives you mighty power, love, and self-control." 2 Timothy 1:7 TPT

Unstoppable

In 2019 my focus word for the year was Unstoppable. I was my biggest enemy. I realized that the only one stopping me was me. That I serve an Unstoppable God and with Him I can scale any wall.

In your strength I can crush an army; with my God I can scale any wall.

Psalm 18:29

First, I had to stop being so critical over myself and change the language of my self-talk. I learned in order to be unstoppable; we have to change our mindsets or in other words our way of thinking. Although I was not the little mixed girl in Madison-Mayodan anymore, I found myself still overcoming a poverty mindset - the thoughts that I do not belong with certain classes of people as a result of where I came from and how I was treated. Rich or poor, we all need God. I now stand in faith and decree that no longer will we be held captive by our thoughts, our past, or the way we were brought up.

Godfidence

On the other side of fear is your purpose. I am praying that you find the confidence in God you need to tackle your fears head on. With God you can take on an army and scale a wall (Psalm 18:29)

77

You do not have to be bound by fear any longer, let us take up our rightful positions as children of God and as warriors and fight the good fight of faith to fulfill His purpose designed for each of us. How can this be, you ask?

Mind Over Matter

2 Corinthians 10:35 says:

"Cast down thoughts and imaginations that exalt themselves against God through the power of the Holy Spirit."

In Matthew 6 we are told to "Take No Thought". Think about that, we have the choice. You can either take the thought or reject it. I am here to tell you that through God and the power of the Holy Spirit your Helper, you have the power to take them captive.

Still thinking you are unworthy?

I for one am not one to dwell on my past. I know that I am not that same girl anymore, however I knew I had to reach back. When I think about all the fear and the shame that kept me quiet and paralyzed for so long, I have to share my story to try to spare someone else years of dealing with the same torment. If you still cannot receive this from me, let us take a look at someone in the Bible. Let us put shame even further to death. Let us consider Rahab in the book of Joshua Chapter 2.

Rahab was known as a young prostitute and some theologians believe she may have run the brothel. Either way it goes although Rahab was not the likely candidate, God chose Rahab to be the one to make a way for the Israelites to ultimately enter into their Promised Land. Her choice could have led to her and her family's death with her city's king; however, she chose to be obedient to God (The King of Kings). God's choice led to her and her family's new life and life more abundantly. As a result, she is mentioned several times throughout the bible in regard to her faith. The one thing that I would like to point out to you is this: In Matthew 1:5 we see that she married a prince that grafted her right into the genealogy of Jesus. How powerful is that?! She became one of Jesus' great grandmothers. Through her One Act of Obedience to God she was redeemed.

See we naturally want to count ourselves out because of all the mistakes we think we have made, but God was not moved by any of that. He saw her heart. He saw her courage. And He knew He could use that. This is exactly what God does with us. Never tell yourself that you are too far away from God,

or that He cannot hear you

or that you are too dirty

or that you have done too much

or that you have been through too much

or that He cannot use you

David said in Psalm 139 "even if I make my bed in hell you are with me and even in darkness I cannot hide from you." Mind over matter – it is time to elevate your thinking. Come on the battle has been real in your mind – it is time to fight back! It is time to take those thoughts and crush them under the feet of Jesus.

Trust > Fear

Fear is a liar. What does not kill you only makes you stronger because it allows us to make room for God. Through it all, I have experienced a lot of highs and lows. Through it all I learned to trust God. I had some serious trust issues as a result of my life experiences and when God instructed me to open the doors of our home as Freedom Ministries

Church & Outreach, He had to show me *ME* prior to
that.

✿

Proverbs 3:3-5 Amplified
Do not let mercy *and* kindness and truth leave you
[instead let these qualities define you];
Bind them [securely] around your neck,
Write them on the tablet of your heart.

So find favor and high esteem
In the sight of God and man.

Trust in *and* rely confidently on the Lord with all
your heart
And do not rely on your own
insight *or* understanding.

By faith and obedience to God we were
ordained by our Apostle friend on August 1, 2010.
Bryan and I both were licensed and ordained as
Pastors. FMCO was founded but we continued
serving our hearts out wherever needed in our
current ministry assignments. You name it, we served

in it. Whether it was administrative duties, cleaning, praise and worship, children's church, youth/teen ministry, intercessory prayer, we loved (and still love) to serve. Over the years, we continued to trust God and seek Him as to when we would actually start Freedom. Trust me, I was not in any rush (smile). In 2012 we found out we were relocating to Charlotte, North Carolina. In January 2013 we took a huge leap of faith and moved to Charlotte. Then Valentine's Weekend February 2014 ("Love Month") we opened up the doors of Freedom right in our dining room.

Prior to becoming a house of ministry, I became a house of worship. True worship is more than just music during a Sunday service and more than just a song or a dance. Worship is a lifestyle. Worship or *worth*-ship is what you value. 1 Peter 5:7 says:

Give all your worries and cares to God, for he cares about you.

We can literally transfer our worries into worship as we take our focus off the distraction and shift it to God. Worship aligns your focus to the

Creator and less on the creation. As I began to trust God and allow God to be in the highest position in my life, He began to bring order. He showed me that I am the heart of the home and if I remain closed off, then everything else does - my family, our ministry, my business, etc. I recently read a quote that said,

"If you don't heal what hurt you, you'll bleed on people who didn't cut you." (Author unknown)

God had to deal with my heart issues, and I had to allow Him to heal me, so that He could make room for the people who were and are still coming through the doors of FMCO. He taught me that I do not have to necessarily trust the people because getting hurt is inevitable at times even as a pastor, we still hurt, but that I can completely trust Him through it all. I keep my heart open now solely in obedience. I have to - it is my *reasonable service* unto God. (Romans 12:1) This once shameful little girl stands today naked and unashamed in His Presence which was His original plan for us all in Genesis 2:25.

I keep my heart open now solely in obedience.

Success Through Obedience

Romans 8:37 says:

"Yet even in the midst of all these things, we triumph over them all, for God has made us to be more than conquerors, and his demonstrated love is our glorious victory over everything!"

Triumph or Success does not always look pretty. You are successful when you overcome something and overcoming something is not always pretty. You have to fight for it. The problem is that success is mostly viewed in our culture as having material wealth and popularity, or we gauge success by seeing the finished product, not ever considering the process it took to get there.

The word success comes from the root word *succedere* which means to **"come after, follow after; go near to; come under; take the place of,"** And here God is saying, <u>**His demonstrated love**</u> **is our glorious victory** (or success) **over everything!**

What exactly is his demonstrated love?

Romans 5:8 **says:**

"God demonstrates His own love toward us, in that while we were still sinners, Christ died for us."

In other words, we are most successful when we:

1. Submit to Jesus and God's Love
2. Draw near to Jesus and God's Love
3. Allow God's Love to take the place of what we deemed as love
4. Share God's Love with others

Take a quick look back over your life. Look at everything you have survived and everything you have conquered - every time you thought you were breaking down, but God came through each time and all the times you made the choice to still love others even though you were hurting. Consider the times you were obedient to God even when the cost was great. We have to stop being so hard on ourselves. We have to give ourselves grace.

God does not measure success the same way that we do - **Man looks at the outward appearance, God looks at the heart (1 Samuel 16:7)**

Remember God's ways are not like our ways nor are His Thoughts like ours (Isaiah 55:8-9).

As a matter of fact, I am convinced that He looks at what we consider to be our biggest personal failures or mistakes as our Greatest Successful Moments, because it is in those moments that our mindsets are broken, and He is able to break through!

Chapter 8

From Commitment Phobic to Fully Committed

Subsequently, I have learned to not measure success as the world does but how God intends. In going deeper in God's Demonstrated Love, I have also learned about humility and forgiveness. We cannot fully commit without first humbling ourselves. You cannot truly ask for forgiveness without humbling yourself first. It is also important to know that forgiveness is not even for the other person, it is most importantly for YOU! Do you remember what I shared earlier about what happens when we build these walls to protect ourselves and that we are also keeping God away from that area? Forgiveness does not necessarily mean that the relationship you had with that person will go back to the way things were, but what it means is that you ask God to help restore you back to the way He intended which was to be loved and to love others. Not necessarily with the love that we have previously come to know.

God's Love or Agape Love is literally translated into Perfectly Perfect Love or Completely Complete Love.

Being Fully Committed requires a greater level of maturity, especially when we are talking about forgiveness and releasing hurts — both relational and church hurts. Prior to opening FMCO, my husband and I served in multiple churches which were great opportunities for learning and growth but there were painful experiences there too.

We love because He first loved us.

Listen, I have done some things (lots of things actually) that I would not dare mention in this book. I have hurt a lot of people as well as I was wrestling with myself and trying to navigate through who I was called to be. There are some testimonies we just do not tell, but God knows, and He still loves you. He still calls you. We have to forgive ourselves and each other as God through Christ forgave us. People are not perfect. Church people are not perfect. Leaders in the church are not perfect. We are not perfect, but once you receive salvation the One who is Perfect resides in you.

Let go of Unrealistic Standards and Expectations

that we hold for people

"Make allowance for each other's faults and forgive anyone who offends you. Remember, the Lord forgave you, so you must forgive others."

Colossians 3:13 NLT

15 All who declare that Jesus is the Son of God have God living in them, and they live in God. 16 We know how much God loves us, and we have put our trust in his love.
God is love, and all who live in love live in God, and God lives in them. 17 And as we live in God, our love grows more perfect. So we will not be afraid on the day of judgment, but we can face him with confidence because we live like Jesus here in this world.
18 Such love has no fear, because perfect love expels all fear. If we are afraid, it is for fear of punishment, and this shows that we have not fully experienced his perfect love. 19 We love each other because he loved us first.

1 John 4:15-19 NLT

In regard to 1 John 4:17, His love being made perfect or perfected in us does not necessarily mean we are being made perfect but mature. Even the most active person you see in a church, their heart could be far from God. So let's not blame God when we experience these hurts especially from believers. Let's not hold God accountable for that part. Some of you reading this right now have been afraid to go back to church as a result of this. These types of hurt hit different because you expect to be hurt in the secular world, but you least expect it inside the church. I know because I have experienced it, too, but child of God I submit to you today, to let that go. God was not in it. Do not hold them and yourself hostage any longer. God's Love versus our love is what is being described in this chapter (1 John 4). The original translation of God's Love or Agape Love is the highest form of love. Agape love means a love that is perfect and complete.

This perfect and complete love drives out all fear (1 John 4:18). Fear involves torment or punishment. The one who fears is not perfected in love. **FEAR = False Evidence Appearing Real.** This type of fear is not the proper fear or reverence for God but fear that involves torment. It is the kind of fear that robs us of our joy and confidence in His PERFECTLY PERFECT LOVE. I recently asked myself this question: "Why is it so hard for us to reach back out for reconciliation especially if there has been some time passed by?" The Holy Spirit revealed to me that it is because that is when our minds begin to speak to us certain thoughts that are not true about the person or about our God. We have got to CONFESS to know and believe as it says in verses 15 and 16. When your mind begins to wonder, Confess PERFECT LOVE DRIVES OUT ALL FEAR!

Most recently verses 20 and 21 hit me pretty hard.
20 If someone says, "I love God," but hates a fellow believer, that person is a liar; for if we don't love people we can see, how can we love God, whom we cannot see? 21 And he has given us this command: Those who love God must also love their fellow believers.
The thing that was bothering me was now that I have been walking in the faith for some time, I did not want to believe that I actually "hated" anyone, however, God took me deeper in His Word and showed me that the original Greek word used here for hate is *Miseō* which literally translates to *Less than* or *Imperfect*. In other words, hatred is Imperfect Love or Less than Love. Beloved, I submit

to you that those who have hurt you (especially those who you loved and thought they loved you) - That was not the true Perfectly Perfect or Completely Complete Love of God in operation.

Being Fully Committed requires a greater level of maturity. Forgiveness. Releasing of hurts. Church hurts.

When I was a child, I spoke about childish matters, for I saw things like a child and reasoned like a child. But the day came when I matured, and I set aside my childish ways.

1 Corinthians 13:11(TPT)

Just because the bible says we are to have child-like faith in Him, this does not give us the okay to act childish when we deal with others. We love each other best when we ask God how to love our brother or sister. His love is being perfected in us when we truly love each other this way.

Anyone can say they Love God because truthfully that cannot be seen, but our love for our brother or sister and how we treat people is seen. We cannot love people in our own strength or in our own love. Our love has limits. Our love has restrictions and

motives. We set these all aside, and ask The One whose Love is Perfectly Perfect to help us love one another that is what John is saying:
To be Fully Committed, we have to humble ourselves. To be fully committed, we have to restore our relationships with God and man. Commitment phobia is a real thing, believe me I know.   John had every right to treat others bad now. Jesus was no longer walking with him in this earth. He could have gone back to being a regular fisherman. He could have put walls up and chose not to deal with people at all and maybe he did for a moment, but he knew too much about him. This applies to us, too! We have a choice too, but we know too much about Him. John's name means God is gracious.   Deep down, we know we are not right and maybe that is what some of us are afraid of. John is reminding us that God is Gracious and wants to restore relationships today in His Love not ours.

Passion

Remember the movie The Passion of The Christ? Remember the cross? Because of God's Great and Passionate Love for us, Jesus Christ died on the cross for our sins. We love because He first loved us, and it is of the utmost importance for us to become passionate about Him again; not only for Him, about the gifts He has given us to use for His glory to reach others. Each and every one of us was put on this planet for a purpose. Now, I do not mean you have to open a church and start preaching. Your purpose could be used right where you are, in your home, school, and/or job. It could be something as simple as sharing your story with someone. Telling them how God's Love is bringing you through. Whether you think your purpose is too big or too small, it is for a Greater Purpose. God's Love is invisible to most people so that is why it is important to show His Love to others.

"Put your heart and soul into every activity you do, as though you are doing it for the Lord himself and not merely for others."

Colossians 3:23 TPT

It is time to become passionate in your relationship with God. If you have already been walking with Him for some time, it is time to reignite the flame.

Have you ever seen newlyweds together? Sure you have. You see how they look at each other? How they want to be near each other constantly? I remember when Bryan and I were first together, we would leave each other and then call as soon as we got home (before cell phones). Then we would not want to hang the phone up. We would fall asleep on the phone together. Now, most of our phone calls are very quick and to the point and if we are honest, we have gotten the same way with God and about the things of God (serving Him with our gifts). We have gotten too comfortable in our relationship with God. Over time this can happen to all of us. And this can change, and it starts with you.

Restore to me the joy of your salvation and make me willing to obey you.

Psalm 51:12 NLT

96

Chapter 9

The Recap

God wants to do so much more in and through us, but we have got to Fully Commit - How?

1. Humility

2. Restoring the Relationship - Be quick to forgive

3. Becoming Passionate in the relationship

Stop and Think

If you are reading this and have never asked Jesus to come into your heart or if you are thinking, "how do I get saved?", it is very simple!

Pray this Prayer with me

Dear Lord Jesus,

I know that I am a sinner. We all are; we all fall short every single day, but I believe You died for my sins and rose from the dead so that I can experience life change. My ways are not working for me and I need You. I need a Savior and I invite you to come into my heart and life. I want to trust you and follow you only. I accept your love. I accept your help.

Welcome to The Kingdom!

Don't Brace Yourself - Grace Yourself

Why is it that we give everyone else so much grace, yet we are so hard on ourselves? Others can do us wrong over and over again, yet we do not give up on them. We mess up once and we give up on ourselves. Stop being so hard on yourself! As you move forward in forgiving yourself, remember to grace yourself - allow yourself room to make mistakes. God is not looking for us to be perfect. He is looking to perfect His Love in us.

The walls we put up in defense to keep ourselves from getting hurt prevents God from getting into that area. Letting your guard down is risky but it is so worth it! Believe me I had serious trust issues! When you finally find the freedom to let your guard down this time, ask God to fill that space. Let Him protect you. Let Him guide you. Are there any areas where you know you need to forgive yourself? Are there any areas where you know you need to let your guard down and allow God to fill that space?

_____

_____

_____

_____

_____

God is Gracious

Now just because we receive salvation, things do not magically go away. We have to walk it out by faith. You have to make the choice. Things that were done without thinking before, can take some time to be undone. It is a process.

I personally have no regrets for how my story went; it ultimately drew me closer to God and made me who I am today. I do not blame anyone. I accept full responsibility for choices and decisions I have made as a result. I choose to forgive others, but most importantly I forgive me. I used the present tense there because this is an everyday process. I am still a work in progress and still trusting God with every step along the way. It is only by His grace that I am still here and in my right mind. As a matter of fact, both of my parents' names mean the exact same thing, "God is gracious". They both point me back to God's grace from my beginning to now.

God has since restored my relationship with my dad. Our relationship got better once I let go of unrealistic expectations I had set for him. I was once a daddy's girl and I had to come to the understanding that I was offended by him solely because I held him so high on this pedestal as if he could do no wrong. He retired from the military and currently resides in Louisiana. He is happily married, a successful entrepreneur, and a servant in ministry. We may not live close to each other, but when we do talk and see each other is when it matters most. I am his first-born daughter and I know that no matter what he loves me.   My mother still mothers like no other. It hurt her the way that she found out about the molestation later in my twenties as I gave my testimony to a crowd of strangers. I know she blamed herself just like any mom would. I know anytime I need anything, she will always be right here. She is so faithful and dependable. She eventually remarried and serves wherever she is needed. She is the best mother I could have and an even greater grandmother to our kids. I do not esteem her nearly as often as I should. I am still working on expressing my love and asking for help. When I think of all the billions of people in this world and how God chooses to connect families together, I could not be more grateful for my parents. They are both less than perfect, but perfectly chosen to steward and guide me on this earth.

I would certainly be remiss if I did not mention Bryan's parents, Ronnie and Gerl - I met them when I was only seventeen years old. They have managed to stay married throughout all of these years and gave me hope that Bryan and I could make it. I ended up with an extra mother and father in Love. They have helped us so much in tough times and are excellent grandparents. I know our parents' combined prayers have carried us through at times. I am who I am today as a result of them and God's Love and Grace. Oh and over the years, God has given me more than I could ever ask or think of in the area of girlfriends. He has connected me with some awesome ladies who are more than friends, they are my sisters. This once closed off heart that vowed to never trust and would push away people who I knew loved me (especially those closest to me) and who was once "Miss Independent" is now totally dependent on God and you can be too. If not for yourself, be the person that you needed when you were younger.

Be the person you needed

Mentorship is important; I think about how different my life might have panned out if I had a mentor or someone to guide me through when I was that broken little girl, but as a result, I learned to trust God and Him alone so that I can reach back and help pull others out of their trenches. The next time you notice someone struggling or 'acting out', please do not judge them, but instead, give them what you needed and be who you needed. Show them love. Give them Grace.

Maybe you have never experienced rejection as a result of your race or how you look. Maybe you are not a Half-Breed racially, however being a half-breed or a misfit can translate into other areas of your life. If you have ever felt like you do not belong or have always struggled to find your place, there is a place for you in God. If you ever felt like you had to walk alone at times and had to figure this whole thing called life out on your own even in church, God is still there. In fact, He is here with you right now as you read this. Think about it, God only created one you. Even if you are a twin or from multiple births, you are still different and there is only one you on this earth that can do what you do. You have purpose.

Just Be You
No matter what color you are
No matter what race
No matter where you are from

I pray you find the confidence to *just be you* - Your true authentic self who God created you to be.

You can just be you. There is something God has placed in you that is meant to introduce others to the saving power of Jesus and it is all on the other side of fear.

But you are A CHOSEN RACE, A royal PRIESTHOOD, A HOLY NATION, A PEOPLE FOR God's OWN POSSESSION, so that you may proclaim the excellencies of Him who has called you out of darkness into His marvelous light 1 Peter 2:9 New American Standard Bible

Keep learning to accept who you are but more importantly *whose* you are. Extend grace to yourself as you begin or continue to run your race. You are going to make an impact in this world. Let's run this race together. No longer worrying about who is not with us - if God is for us, who can stand against us (Romans 8:31)? Again, you are not alone. We can be successful at navigating this world as we take back our rightful places in The Kingdom of God. We can live as victorious "Half-Breeds" in Him.

Even if you do not have a mentor or someone to show you how, you still have a purpose. Some things, He never intended to be manmade or for other people to get the credit for. Some things He wants to be the only One to get the glory from. My husband and I did not come through a religious vein and that is okay. There are people waiting on you to stand up and take your place, so that you can help them out. As church planters, we have often felt like outcasts when it comes to religious-related things. God wants a relationship with us more than our works, religion, and service. Honestly, with God and the Holy Spirit as our covering and not man at times it gets rough. We are not perfect, and we still make mistakes, but God's grace continues to cover us and shine through us even more in those moments.

Remember His Strength is made perfect in our weaknesses. He is not looking for us to be perfect. He is perfect and created us to need Him because He knew us even before time began. The longing to be love can only be fulfilled by Him.

※

"My grace is all you need. My power works best in weakness." So now I am glad to boast about my weaknesses, so that the power of Christ can work through me.

2 Corinthians 12:9 NLT

I was set apart!

The separation or moments of abandonment I experienced from people was God's way of setting me a part. He was always there even when I could not feel Him. I know now that I am never alone.

The years of depression, anxieties, sorrow, loss of motivation - I had to overcome these things. I have to choose to fight for my life and freedom from myself every day. Much like how my cousin Christine came to fight for me that day, that is exactly how The Lord fights for us. We never know what He is keeping back from us. He only allows certain tests and/or trials to get to us that He knows will not crush us. Yes a lot of our battles are from our own choices, however He still extends His grace to us in that.

Behold, I give unto you power to tread on serpents and scorpions, and over all the power of the enemy: and nothing shall by any means hurt you - Luke 10:19

I do not know about you, but snakes terrify me. I never knew exactly how much I feared them until one got into my house somehow a few years ago. So this scripture holds even more power to me now since that incident. If you look closer, you will see that God is also speaking to us on another level here about the two creatures. He mentions both snakes and scorpions, while both are creepy (especially to me) they have another thing in common. They both inject a deadly venom into their prey.

John 10:10 says:

"The thief comes only to steal and kill and destroy; I came that they may have life and have *it* abundantly".

How does the enemy wage this war? He targets our minds. Most of the time, our adversary's venom of choice is either paralyzing fear or the stumbling block of offense. In other words, we can choose to be offended and blind ourselves from the truth of God or we can choose to Live and not only live but live on purpose. Sometimes a shift in perspective is all we need.

God is not concerned about our comfort more than He is concerned about our hearts and our healing.

As a matter of fact, He never said the serpents and scorpions would not come. He basically said when they do come, "*I have given you power!*" I recall a vivid memory of when I was a little girl playing outside of my Great Grandma Katherine's house, I saw a snake and I frantically ran inside to tell her. I watched this great woman of faith and strength grab a gardening hoe and she so confidently and boldly found the snake and chopped his head off. That is how we should be in God. See, these things in our life (snakes, scorpions, trauma, tribulations, etc.) come to shift us. When we focus on our strength, we tend to fear or take sides with the worst that could happen. On the other hand, when we focus on His strength, we are reminded that we can do all things through Christ who strengthens us and that nothing is impossible with God. **(Philippians 4:13, Matthew 19:26, Luke 1:37)**

"God has answered me"

I am married today with my husband for almost two decades, people said we would never last, and only God can get the glory. Together we are raising three strong young black men and one beautiful daughter whose name is literally translated into *"God has answered me with Grace"*. The way my story went, it did not end there. Please do not feel sorry for me. I am not a victim in any way! I am chosen and graced for the call. I did not ask for any of this, it is all according to His Plan. I have learned that trials and tribulations will still come, but how you respond is what truly counts. This *Half-Breed* chooses to Graciously, God-fidently (read as full confidence in God), and Victoriously keep making steps forward in my journey to Freedom knowing full well that I was created for purpose, I am *graced for this* life I have been given, and I have an even greater ending to still achieve.

Flip the Script

Now that we have gotten to the root of our issues, it is time to flip them to advance the Kingdom of God. Ask yourself and God this –

In what ways, can I use the serpents and scorpions from my past to help others?

Now Go Forth!

[13] I don't depend on my own strength to accomplish this; however I do have one compelling focus: I forget all of the past as I fasten my heart to the future instead. [14] I run straight for the divine invitation of reaching the heavenly goal and gaining the victory-prize through the anointing of Jesus. [15] So let all who are fully mature have this same passion, and if

anyone is not yet gripped by these desires, God will reveal it to them.

Philippians 3:13-15 (TPT)

"Free to Be Me"
(excerpt from my personal blog "*Grace to Speak*")

For many years I was never comfortable in my own skin. Too black for white kids, too white for black. I spent several years trying to find my place, however, today is a different day! I thank God for the freedom to be able to be comfortable with the image staring back at me in the mirror. Christ is the only one who understands the years of rejection, hurt, and abuse. It is through Him, that I now understand that True Beauty is way more than skin deep. It is a heart thing. A heart at rest is the most beautiful thing a person could ever have. No more striving or people pleasing! I am now living life on purpose, I am now free!

To this day I am still asked the dreaded question, "Where are you from?" in other words, WHAT ARE YOU??!!! Now I can truly smile and graciously respond that I am Jackie from a small town called Madison-Mayodan, NC. I am mixed/bi-racial/a half-breed. My Dad is black, my Mom is white, and I am beautiful, Beautifully Me.

About the Author

Pastor Jackie Lowe is a native of Madison-Mayodan, North Carolina (a true Country Girl to say the least). Upon surrendering her heart to God, she has served in various areas of ministry including: the Intercessory Prayer Team, in Praise and Worship, with Prophetic Dance, and Youth Pastor.

She is married to her Best Friend, Pastor Bryan Lowe. November 2020 will mark nineteen years of blissful marriage for she and Pastor Bryan. Together, they have 4 wonderful children (3 boys and 1 baby girl).

Pastors Bryan and Jackie were ordained in August 2010, and with God's direction, Freedom Ministries Church and Outreach (FMCO) was founded. In February 2014, FMCO opened its doors in Charlotte, North Carolina where she currently resides with her family.

She is not only known as Pastor Jackie, but also as a loving daughter, great friend, and a North Carolina Realtor. Her education includes studying Psychology and Christian Counseling at Liberty University. Pastor Jackie Lowe is truly a Woman after God's Heart; she loves you right where you are, to get you where you need to go.

Her Life Verse is Luke 1:45, which reads:

"Blessed is she who has believed

that the Lord would fulfill His promises to her!"

www.ingramcontent.com/pod-product-compliance
Lightning Source LLC
Chambersburg PA
CBHW052044270326
41931CB00012B/2617